BACKYARDS
and Butterflies

Ways to Include Children with Disabilities in Outdoor Activities

Doreen Greenstein, Ph.D.
Cornell University

Naomi Miner, O.T.R./L.
Assistive Technology Design
Clinical Consultant

Emilie Kudela, M.Ed.
Technical Writer

Suzanne Bloom, B.F.A.
Illustrator

 **Brookline Books**

Technical Review

Carol Anderson — Associate Director, Cornell Cooperative Extension, Cornell University

Sally Barney — Extension Specialist, University of New Hampshire

Maurice W. Dorsey — State Program Leader, University of the District of Columbia

Bari S. Dworken — Extension Educator Coordinator, Camping, University of Connecticut

Ronald Kujawski — Landscape and Nursery Specialist, University of Massachusetts

Pamela Marshall — Extension Agent, Agriculture and Natural Resources, University of the District of Columbia

Shirley Mietlicki — Family Life Education, University of Massachusetts

Ben H. Nolt, Jr. — Coordinator, 4-H Therapeutic Riding Program, Penn State University

Jan Scholl — Assistant Professor of Agriculture and Extension Education, Penn State University

Charles V. Schwab — Safety Specialist, Iowa State University

Tom Waskiewicz — 4-H Program Coordinator, University of Massachusetts

Printed, 1995.

Library of Congress Cataloging-in-Publication Data
Backyards and butterflies: ways to include children with
    disabilities in outdoor activities / Doreen Greenstein ...
    [et al.]
      p.   cm.
    ISBN 1-57129-001-7 (pbk.)
    1. Outdoor recreation for handicapped children.
2. Outdoor recreation--Equipment and supplies.
I. Greenstein, Doreen.
GV191.635.B33   1995
796'.0196--dc20   95-22965
                                                  CIP

Available from
BROOKLINE BOOKS
P.O. Box 1047
Cambridge, MA 02238
1-800-666-BOOK

This material is based upon work supported by the Extension Service, United States Department of Agriculture. The text is available in electronic format.

Heather Allen, layout

Copyright © 1993.

CONTENTS

OUR GARDEN ....Page 8

Locating an accessible garden 8
Raised beds 9
Barrels, plastic bags, and other
   places to plant 9
An accessible plant table 10
Planting buckets 11
Bean tepee 11
Choosing what to plant 12

Help with planting seeds 12
Holding a garden hose 13
Trowel 13
One-handed hoe 14
Easy-grip watering can 14
Carrying and storing garden
   tools 15
Insert seat 15

NATURE ....Page 18

Homemade tents 18
Feeding birds 18
Thinking about pond safety 20
Pond accessibility 20
Adapting pond "stuff" 20
Studying pond critters 21
Collections 21

Picking and holding wildflowers ...22
Berry picking 23
Accessibility in the berry patch 23
Catching insects 24
Insect houses 24
Looking at insects 25

ANIMALS ....Page 28

Accessibility concerns 28
An accessible rabbit hutch 28
Grooming 29
Putting on boots 30
Feeding and watering chickens 31
Feed scoop 31

Easy-grip calf bottle 32
Caring for the family dog 32
Horseback riding 33
Custom-made riding aids 33
N.A.R.H.A. 34
4-H involvement for your child 34

WHEELS ....Page 38

Tricycles 38
Vertical tricycle handlebar grips 38
Tricycle pedal foot holders 39
An electric tricycle 39
Commercial electric cars 40
Permanent support wheels 41

Walker/wagon 42
Scooter board 43
Wagon insert seat 43
A word about wheels and tires 44
Safety precautions 44
Ground surfaces 44

SWINGS & SLIDES ....Page 48

Safety issues 48
Slide with ramp 49
Hillside slide 50
Sandbox 50
Swings 51

Swing hardware 51
Hammock swing 51
Four-sided ladder 52
Car seat swing 54

OUR BACKYARD ....Page 58

The back porch 58
Ramp specifications in rural
    settings 58
Ramps in snowy and wet
    climates 59
Handrails on ramps 59

Fences: types and uses 59
Accessible picnic table 60
Picnic table extension 61
Swivel seat for picnic table .. 62
Adirondack chair 63
Inclusion/Conclusion 64

MEASUREMENTS & MATERIALS ....Page 65

Measurements 65
Materials 66
Balls 66
Bolts/screws/nuts/washers .. 66
Buckets/containers/scoops .. 67
Dowels 67
Glues 68
Handles/knobs 68
Lumber/plywood 68
Pipe insulation 68

Plastic 69
Radiator hose clamps 69
Silicone caulking, and non-slip
    surfaces 69
Tie wraps 70
Velcro 70
Waterproof tape 71
Webbing 71
Wire 71

This book was written by four mothers sitting around a kitchen table. Besides being mothers, we are also a developmental psychologist, an occupational therapist, a special educator, and an illustrator. Most of the ideas in the book have been thought of, and made, by parents. Others have been made by us, for children we've worked with. The walker-wagon has been on a wild turkey hunt (carrying stale bread and a length of rope with which to capture a turkey that was heard gobbling in the woods.) The hammock swing has been swung on, the rungs of the four-sided ladder swing have been darkened to a patina by grubby hands....

This book is for children. We are sharing rural children's experiences with you. We do not exclude urban and suburban children, but when we write about picking daisies along a roadside, we are reflecting our experiences, and the experiences of rural families with whom we work. In each chapter we share ideas on making outdoor environments more accessible and safer for ALL children.

This book is for parents. We are communicating ideas by parents and for parents. We do not exclude professionals as readers, but we do ask that professionals wear their "parent hats." The ideas presented in this book have, in large part, been thought of by rural parents, whose children, for whatever reason, have needed special accommodations in order to fully enjoy outdoor activities.

This book is for families. We are writing a "how-to" book for families. We do not exclude schools or therapeutic programs as audiences, but our goal is to make our children's home environments as accessible as their school environments. These are low-tech, inexpensive, homemade "assistive technology" ideas for use at home.

How to use this book. Use these ideas as a starting point; change them to meet your special family needs. Involve your children in designing the projects, selecting the materials, and making the items with you. Use whatever materials you have around. Make prototypes and refine your ideas. And — when you have solved your unique problems, send your solutions to us! We'd love this to be an ongoing process. More ideas — more books. More books — more ideas....

S.BLOOM '93

OUR GARDEN

Gardening is an important part of life for many families. Children love to share in the work and the rewards of gardening. In fact, they're usually the ones who notice the first flower buds and the first ripe vegetables. By offering ideas in this chapter that will make gardening more accessible we hope every child will be able to join in the fun of gardening.

Gardens provide so many experiences for children: planning, purchasing seeds, planting, watching the miracle of growth, cultivating, and, literally, enjoying the fruits of their labor! Children love to dig and plant, and feel a sense of accomplishment regardless of how well the plants grow. Every garden experience teaches a lesson. Was the garden watered often enough? Did the plants get enough sunlight? When your child helps in the garden, every ripened vegetable, every fully opened flower, is like a blue ribbon prize.

Gardening starts long before summer, when seed catalogs arrive in late winter. At that time, you and your child can start planning your garden, and in early spring you can both plant seeds indoors for transplanting later. If gardening is new to you, keep your project small and simple so it won't frustrate your child (or you!) Your county Cooperative Extension Service offers workshops and fact sheets that will help you get started.

Choose hand tools that fit your child's size and make sure the tools are sturdy. Most children prefer to use real "grown-up" tools. If the handles are too long, shorten them by cutting off the end of the handle, and sand the end or wrap tape around it for safety.

Locating an accessible garden

The best location for an accessible garden is near your house so that it can be visited easily. If possible, the accessible part of the garden should be an integrated part of the family garden so that everyone can work together. Start off with basic garden requirements and then add modifications for your child's special needs and interests. Your child should help as much as possible in garden preparation and modification plans.

Select a well-drained area, and be sure the ground surface of your garden spot is level. Remove any protruding stones and rake the pathways until the surface is smooth. Allow at least 36 inches width for wheelchair paths and 60 inches in diameter for wheelchair turn-arounds. You can build pathways with boards by lining up two rows of flat scrap lumber end to end, spacing the rows to match the distance between the wheels of the wheelchair. Accessible pathways can also be made of plywood sheets, old cow mats, conveyor belting, or anything else that provides a smooth surface. Look around your yard or neighborhood for inexpensive surfacing material.

Raised beds

Raised beds are garden areas filled with soil and enclosed by stacked landscape timbers. They allow greater access to a planting area. There may be concerns about the chemicals used to treat the wood and the possibility of these chemicals leaching into the soil and the plants. Some treated wood might not be good to use for vegetable plantings. Be sure to ask about the type of chemical treatment and if it is safe to use in a vegetable garden. You can also use untreated boards or scrap lumber. Traditional raised beds may be difficult to use for a child sitting in a wheelchair. Children's legs can be uncomfortably obstructed by the wall, and it is often difficult to maintain good positioning for children who are working in raised beds. Sometimes creating a raised bed of small dimension gives

children easier access to a planting area. A small raised bed can be made by stacking old tires, drilling holes through the sidewalls, bolting each layer to the layer beneath it, and then filling the stack with garden soil. The height of the tire bed should allow for a comfortable forward reach from either a seated or standing position, whichever you choose.

Barrels, plastic bags, and other places to plant

Although we have not included it in our color illustration, another kind of planter is an old wooden barrel. Frequently, these barrels are used to grow strawberries, tomatoes, and vine crops. Cut out circles two inches in diameter along the sides of the barrel. Once the barrel is filled with soil, your child can place plants in each opening. Vegetables have also been grown successfully in plastic trash bags. When you fill the bag with soil, leave some room at the top. The extra plastic can be used to protect young plants from frost. You can find out about using barrels and plastic bags at your local garden store or Cooperative Extension Service.

An accessible plant table

A plant table may be an excellent alternative for a child sitting in a wheelchair. The plant table in our drawing is made of treated lumber and allows the child to get comfortably close to the planting area. The planting areas are large plastic dishpans (really big ones can be purchased at restaurant supply stores) that have been set into a durable, plywood table. First, measure the dishpans and design a frame large enough to hold them. Make a simple table with 4" x 4" legs, sides made of scrap lumber, and a table top made from outdoor plywood (with some drainage holes drilled in it). Also drill several small drainage holes in each dishpan.

Fill the dishpans with garden soil. They can be used to start plants indoors and can be moved outdoors when the weather is warm. Plant varieties with shallow roots. Make sure that your child's wheelchair can fit comfortably underneath the table so your child can reach the soil. For safety, cover all protruding nails on the plant table.

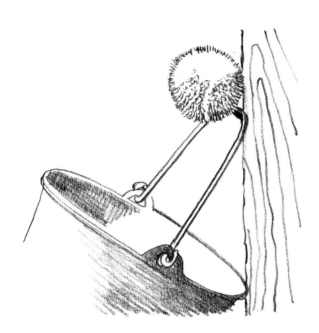

Planting buckets

Additional planting buckets or pots can hang from the plant table within easy reach. Cover the protruding nail with a slit tennis ball as shown in our drawing. Try growing herbs in these buckets. Commercially purchased hanging flower pots have the advantage of having drip catchers but you can use any containers that are not too heavy. A good container is a five gallon plastic bucket that once stored food. (See Materials chapter for information about where to get these buckets.) You can drill holes in the bucket's bottom for drainage.

Bean tepee

Climbing plants that form a natural canopy always seem to fascinate young gardeners. The plants' leaves, flowers, and beans, can be viewed from all sides. Children can even crawl inside the tepee. Make sure the tepee is sturdy so that children can explore safely. The bean plants become quite heavy as they grow; so use at least three heavy duty, well anchored, poles. You can use store-bought poles, tree saplings or branches. Lean the poles inward to form the tepee. Secure the top of the tepee with heavy twine or wire.

When you purchase your bean seeds, be sure they are pole beans and not bush beans. "Kentucky Wonder" and "Blue Lake" pole beans are good varieties to plant. "Scarlet Runner" beans are also a good type of bean to plant because the vines are large, the flowers are bright red, and the beans are tasty. Plant about six seeds at the base of each pole.

Choosing what to plant

Good instructions for planting seeds are found on the back of seed packets. Whether your child can read or not, it is important to point out that directions for planting are there and that different plant varieties have different planting needs. Choose large seeds because they can be seen and handled more easily. Try beans, squash, peas, melons, and onion sets. Easy flower seeds to plant include sunflowers and nasturtiums. For children who tend to put small items in their mouths buy seeds that have not been treated with preservatives. Children who are visually impaired enjoy growing fragrant plants. Try a few varieties of easy-to-grow aromatic herbs, or plant some marigolds with your vegetables. Basil is very easy to grow, or experiment with different mints.

Help with planting seeds

Planting small seeds such as lettuce is more difficult but not impossible. Mix the seeds with some fine soil and pour them from a small necked bottle or paper cup. You can easily make a planting helper, using the bottom half of an egg carton. Cut off the tip of each of the egg holders to form funnels to place seeds in. The child can also pour a bit of small seed and soil mixture into each opening in the carton. For seeds that can be planted in close rows, use the entire bottom part of the egg carton for two rows of neatly planted seeds. Another type of planting helper can be made by cutting one- to two-inch diameter holes in a straight line along a flat board. Place the board on the soil and let your child place the seeds in each opening. Seed tapes are available from some catalogs and seed stores. They are more expensive than loose seeds but are easier to handle. The seeds are attached to tape and eliminate the need for spacing of seeds or thinning the plants later.

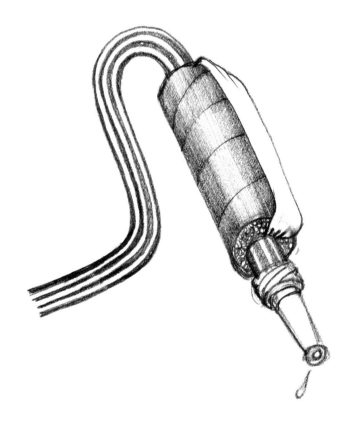

Holding a garden hose

An easy-grip handle for a hose can be made using elastic and pipe insulation. The pipe insulation should fit snugly around the hose. A four inch piece of insulation, 1-1/2 inches in diameter with a 1/2 inch hole opening fits most hoses. Make a strap by inserting a one-inch wide piece of elastic inside the hose insulation opening, tying the ends of the elastic together. Make sure the elastic is comfortably loose on your child's hand. Slide the pipe insulation and elastic over the hose and tape with waterproof tape. To use, place the handle in your child's palm and slide your child's hand under the elastic.

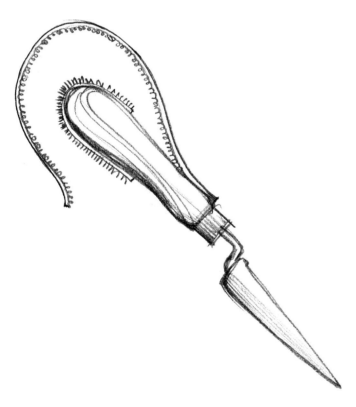

Trowel

Children love to dig with a trowel because the tool is small, easy to handle, and lets the digger get close to the work at hand! For a child who has difficulty grasping a handle, a Velcro strap can help to secure the trowel in the child's hand. Position your child's hand on the trowel handle and make marks on both sides of the hand. (If you are adapting a full-size tool and your child's hand is very small, you may need to measure further up the handle.) Glue the hooked side of a Velcro strip (1-1/2" wide) from the pinky-side mark around the bottom of the trowel handle. Glue the corresponding loop side of the Velcro to the top of the handle from the thumb-side mark as shown in our picture, forming a strap.

This type of Velcro strap can also be used with other small hand tools. If the Velcro is snug on the hand, it makes a secure tool handle without requiring any grasping strength. See "Measurements and Materials" for additional Velcro and gluing suggestions.

One-handed hoe

A hoe, rake, or other garden tool, can be adapted for one-handed use with a discarded forearm crutch. Remove the bottom part of the crutch by releasing the pins that hold it in place. Replace the bottom part of the crutch with a hoe. To determine the best length for the hoe, position the crutch on your child's arm. Make a mark on the ground about 20" in front of your child. Temporarily tape the hoe and crutch together. Have your child reach forward so that the head of the hoe touches the 20" line as you adjust the length of the hoe appropriately. Mark the right length on the hoe handle. Cut off the hoe handle about three inches higher than the mark so it can be inserted into the bottom portion of the crutch. You may need to taper the wooden hoe handle a bit in order to insert it. Secure the crutch to the handle by screwing wood screws through the original pin openings.

Easy-grip watering can

Build up a watering can handle by covering it with pipe insulation and wrapping it with waterproof tape. Or, for an easy alternative to a heavy watering can, use large-sized plastic dish detergent bottles with squirt tops and handles. Children can either hold the bottle in both hands and squeeze, or, if they are able to grip the handle while supporting the container, they can pour from them. Detergent bottles can be easily used from a sitting position. Since they only hold a small amount of water, it may be helpful to fill several containers in advance.

← —20"— →

Carrying, storing garden tools

A bag of washable fabric can be attached to a walker or a wheelchair with Velcro. There are also many good commercially available patterns for handmade bags and kids' aprons so that hand tools, seed packets, and other equipment can be more easily carried.

You may wish to have a more permanent storage container available within your child's reach at the garden spot. Tools and supplies that would be affected by wind or rain can be stored inside. In our color illustration, we show an old metal mailbox attached to the plant table. You can also use a small plastic trash-can, a five-gallon plastic bucket with a lid, or any handy container you have.

Insert seat

In our color illustration, we included a picture of a child sitting in a homemade insert seat. Usually purchased through specialty suppliers, you can build a good seat yourself for backyard use. We want to stress the importance of consulting with your child's occupational or physical therapist if you are going to make a custom-made seat for your child, especially about the correct angles for your child's shoulders and hips. Talk about leg placement and separation. Discuss appropriate support straps and padding. Plywood is a good material to use because it is lightweight, easy to work with, can be glued and screwed together, smoothly sanded, and painted in your child's favorite colors.

We will also show the usefulness of homemade insert seats in other chapters, where we will show them being used in an express wagon, and as a picnic table seat. If you're going to use an insert seat as an actual "insert" rather than a stand-alone chair, make sure you secure it with four bolts that extend through the seat and the surface you're attaching it to.

S.BLOOM '93

NATURE

Maybe it's because little children are so close to the ground that they find so many treasures when they're exploring; it sure seems that all children love pond critters and bugs, birds and animals, flowers and pebbles. Rural children are lucky. They can enjoy nature without having to travel long distances to get to the country! Back-yards can be wonderful places to explore nature.

You don't have to be a science expert to share the excitement of nature with your child. Rachel Carson, a famous naturalist said that "it's not half as important to know as to feel," and part of the fun can be learning about nature together with your child. If you need information, there are many excellent nature books to help you learn the names of everything you may encounter. For suggestions about age-appropriate books, ask at your public library, or browse through your local bookstore.

Children are natural explorers, but the adaptive equipment that some children rely on can interfere with getting close to nature. Walkers and wheelchairs, for example, can be very frustrating to navigate on rough ground. In this chapter, we will give you some suggestions about making nature a bit more accessible for your child. We want to show you that children don't need fancy equipment or sophisticated interventions to interact with nature.

Homemade tents

Something as ordinary as a back-yard tent can provide hours of enjoyment. A tent can be set up for hidden observations of birds, or as a shelter from the hot sun. At night, your child can lie in the tent and watch the wonder of the stars. In our color illustration, we simply hung a blanket over a clothesline (and held the edges down). An old plastic table cloth or shower curtain placed on the ground will help keep the moisture from dampening blankets or sleeping bags in this homemade tent.

Feeding Birds

Birds are a lot of fun to watch, but they can be hard for a child to locate in a tree or bush. A good solution to making elusive birds easier to observe is to hang up a bird feeder. You can attach a container for birdseed on a pole, hang it from a tree, or fasten it to a window frame. If you attach a rope and a pulley to a bird feeder, then

hang it from a tree, your child can help refill it.

Birds also like to eat suet. You can buy it cheaply at the grocery store, or cut off the extra fat from beef and freeze it (so it won't spoil). Place these scraps in a nylon bag such as one used to hold onions, and hang the bag from a tree. Please remember that birds will get used to coming to your backyard to eat, so, once you start feeding birds, we hope you'll continue, especially in bad weather!

Thinking about pond safety

Ponds, swamps, and streams are common features of many rural landscapes, and with or without our permission, children are attracted to these environments. So it is important to think about ways you can make these environments safe for children. Playing near water requires adult supervision and rules for children. Life jackets should be worn at all times when children are playing near water. If you have a pond on your property, look for children's life jackets at rummage sales, and keep a variety of sizes available for visiting children. Make it a rule in your house that all children must wear life jackets if they play anywhere near the pond.

Don't forget to protect children from excessive exposure to the sun while they are playing near the water. Besides the usual hat and sun screen, you may want to attach an inexpensive umbrella (with a clamp on the handle) to your child's wheelchair, in order to create some needed shade.

Pond accessibility

Children love to splash in water, or squish their feet in mud, but if your pond is surrounded on all sides by thick vegetation, it may be difficult for your child to get down to the water's edge. It may be possible for you to cover the pond's bank with washed gravel, forming a beach so that children can easily approach the water. Or, perhaps, a portion of the surrounding grass can be mown short. Turfgrass is an excellent choice. Refer to the "Ground Surfaces" section in the "Wheels" chapter for additional suggestions.

An accessible dock and ramp can also be constructed. Plans for docks are available from your Cooperative Extension Service. If you want to plan for accessibility, make sure that the dock's dimensions are adequate for wheelchair users. See the ramp specifications in our "Backyard" chapter for wheelchair accessibility dimensions.

Adapting pond "stuff"

Simple adaptations can be made to many water toys and playthings. Use your imagination. For example, we suggest lengthening a regular fishing net's handle by attaching a wooden dowel to the handle so that a child can catch frogs and other pond critters while sitting in a wheelchair. The

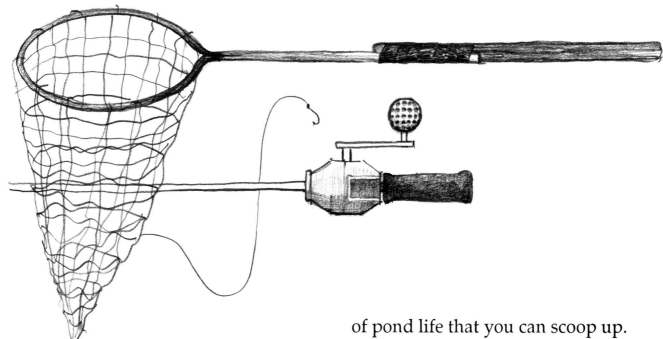

dowel can be attached with waterproof tape or tie wraps.

For some people, a favorite pond activity is fishing. In our drawing we show an adapted fishing pole for a child who has trouble grasping the small handle on the reel. You can cut a small slit in a plastic golf ball and place the ball over the handle so that the handle is inserted snugly in the slit of the ball. If your family is serious about fishing and your child cannot use a regular fishing reel, electric reels and reel holders are commercially available .

Studying pond critters

A fascinating pond project is to fill a gallon jar with pond water, some pond weeds, and mud from the pond bottom. You will be amazed at the variety of pond life that you can scoop up. School cafeterias and restaurants buy mayonnaise and pickles in wide-mouth gallon jars that make wonderful temporary aquariums. Gallon jars are also perfect for tadpoles. Be sure to keep the jar lid off so that there is enough air.

Collections

This is a good place to talk about collecting plants and other living things — about what to keep them in, and whether to keep them at all! Children love to collect things, and making nature collections can be very enjoyable. Leaves and flowers can be pressed between the pages of a book and then made into window displays or scrapbooks. (Old telephone books are good for pressing plants, because the pages are large and the paper isn't glossy.) Egg cartons, or other divided containers, can easily house a rock collection.

It is important for us to teach our children that wild living creatures should be handled as little as possible. While it is enjoyable to catch and observe them for awhile, insects and other animals should be set free after a few hours. Children should also be taught that there are some plants (poison ivy and poison oak, for example) and animals that may be dangerous to touch.

Picking and holding wildflowers

Let's not forget the enjoyment of picking bouquets of common wildflowers. Of course, it goes without saying that we are not in favor of picking the less common flowers, but what is sweeter than to see a child clutching a bouquet of daisies? There are many commercially available children's scissors with metal cutting edges that are adequate for cutting flower stems. If cutting is a problem for your child, many types of stems are easily broken. Some children may need a lot of help from an adult, so it may be a "let's pick flowers together" activity.

For transporting picked wildflowers, we suggest using our spill-proof "vase," made from a plastic soda-pop bottle. Cut off the top section of a one liter soda bottle and insert the top part into the bottom part. Tape the edge all the way around, and pour an inch of water in the bottle. You can attach a handle of wire and pipe insulation, or tape the "vase" to your child's wheelchair or walker. Flower stems are easily inserted into the vase and can be pushed down so that their ends are in the water.

Berry picking

Berry picking is a favorite activity for most children. Wild berries can be hard to get to for children who have difficulty getting around on rough terrain, but cultivated berries are often readily available. Strawberries may be easiest to pick because they are at ground level, easy to see, and have no thorns.

Accessibility in the berry patch

Raspberries, blackberries, and blueberries can be picked more easily from a wheelchair than strawberries. One solution to strawberry picking and accessibility is to go to a U-Pick strawberry farm and ask to pick in the first or last row. You are not going to crush or damage adjacent rows if your child scoots around at the edge of a strawberry field. For children who cannot hold on to the common berry baskets that are made from paper or cardboard, use a shallow pan or a small pail, with a handle that is easy to grip. For one-handed bush berry picking, suspend a small berry bucket from your child's belt. A simple pail can be made from a plastic container by poking two holes near the top and attaching a wire handle. Bush berries can be picked from a wheelchair if the aisles between the rows are moderately flat.

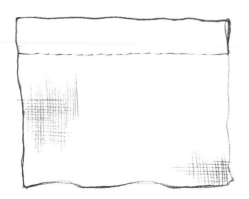
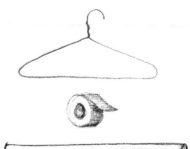
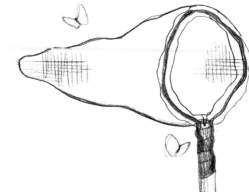

Catching insects

You can capture a surprising number of insects by sweeping an insect net through tall grasses or weeds. A simple net can be made out of a sturdy wire coat hanger, a wooden dowel, and a piece of old nylon curtain material. Bend the coat hanger into a circle. Wrap the hem edge of the curtain around the hanger and cut it to fit the size of the circle. Sew the curtain into the shape of a tapered tube. Unwind the twisted part of the hanger, and thread one end of the wire through the hem of the curtain. Wrap waterproof tape around the wire ends of the coat hanger and the wooden dowel. This type of net can be used in ponds as well as to capture insects.

Insect houses

Insects, if handled gently, can be fascinating temporary "pets." Containers to house insects can be made in several ways. The simplest method is to cover the mouth of a plastic jar with a piece of netting or thin fabric. If it will fit, you can screw on a canning jar lid to hold the material in place; or secure the material with a rubber band placed tightly around the neck of the jar.

You can easily build a sturdy insect house from lumber scraps and screening. Use a piece of wood for the base, and attach, with nails or glue, two smaller pieces of wood for the ends. Before fastening the pieces together, cut a square opening in one end, and attach a piece of heavy cardboard or thin plywood for use as a door, using a screw or bolt to form the door's pivot. Glue an easy-to-grasp handle, such as an empty spool of thread onto the door.

To cover the frame, staple a wide strip of screening into place. If you are using metal screening, make sure you tape the rough edges. Take a strip of scrap molding or narrow board and attach it to the top of the insect house. You can attach a handle to this strip to make carrying easier.

Looking at insects

Remove the insects carefully from the net and place them in one of your insect containers. Remember to provide some foliage for the insect. Try to get some of the same leaves or branches that the insect was on when it was caught. A magnifying glass may help your child see small details. There are magnifiers with their own stands that don't have to be held by hand. If you want to slow the insects' movements so that they can be more easily observed, put the insects and the container in the refrigerator for a few minutes. Because insects are cold blooded, the cold temperature in the refrigerator will make them sluggish and easier to study. But please don't forget them in there! After you and your child have observed the insects for a little while, it's time to let them go. Try to release them in the same vicinity as the one in which they were found.

ANIMALS

Caring for animals can be a rewarding experience for people of almost any age and ability. Children can gain a valuable sense of responsibility by owning pets or helping care for family animals. There are many, many different animals your child can care for; our color illustration provides just a few examples. The ideas in this book can be adapted for the care of other animals. Your local Cooperative Extension office can provide detailed information on selecting and caring for farm animals and backyard pets. Caring for and showing an animal can also be a wonderful 4H project for your child. Cooperative Extension also has inexpensive plans for building shelters for animals.

Your child's abilities and age will determine the appropriate choice of pet or animal, so choosing the right animal, and deciding how caregiving responsibilities are assigned should be a joint decision between parent and child. Keep in mind that placing unrealistic expectations on a child can be frustrating for parents and children alike. Remember, the animal is the one most likely to suffer from inattention or mishandling. So, please plan carefully. Your local humane society (S.P.C.A.) can be very helpful when it comes to selecting appropriate pets.

Accessibility concerns

When you are deciding on the best location for each animal's living quarters, careful planning may make it easier for your child to accomplish more caregiving tasks. For example, for children who are visually impaired, you might want to include guide rails along pathways or outline doors to animal houses and other entranceways with fluorescent paint or tape. Wind chimes can serve as an auditory guidepath for children who are visually impaired. They can be store-bought or homemade.

Take into consideration your child's physical abilities and the animal's needs. For example, place your dog's house near an accessible pathway to your house so that your child's wheelchair can reach it easily. If you need to create pathways to reach the animals, appropriate ground surfaces have been discussed in other chapters.

An accessible rabbit hutch

The rabbit hutch is adapted from a Cornell Cooperative Extension plan (Hutches for Rabbits #6137). To make the design more useful to our readers, we've included a few extra features. Support the hutch with four 2"x4" posts high enough so that your child's wheelchair can fit underneath the front of the hutch. Place a tray or piece of sheet metal underneath the wire floor of the hutch, tilted so that rabbit droppings are directed toward the back of the hutch. Wrap the edge of the tray with waterproof tape to prevent cuts. Similarly, cover all other sharp edges or protruding nails. Make all handles and latches large enough so they can be seen and gripped easily. The hay manger and water bottle can be filled easily from outside. This design enables a child to use the handles and latches from a sitting position. You can order simple rabbit hutch plans from your Cooperative Extension office, and incorporate the changes suggested here, as well as others that you think of.

Grooming

Our color illustration also includes a child grooming a pet rabbit using a hairbrush with a built-up handle. Almost any regular grooming brush or comb can be easily modified using pipe insulation and waterproof tape, with Velcro or elastic strapping (see the hose handle in our Garden chapter).

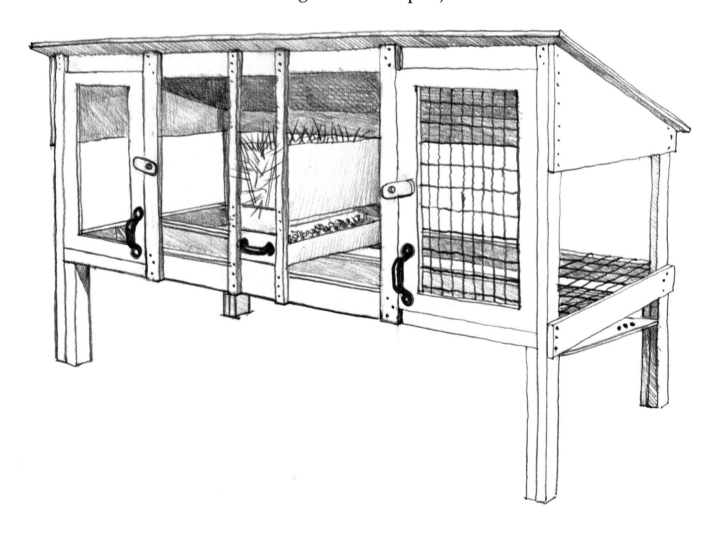

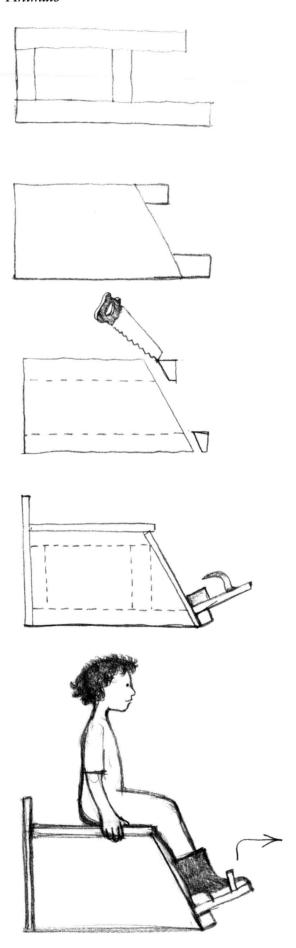

Putting on boots

Boots and muddy yards go together. When it's hard for children to put on their own rubber boots, a boot bench may help. It is a plywood bench with a shelf that holds the boots with a Velcro strap and heel holders. We made the heel holders from a small, round, plastic freezer container that we sawed in half. When the boots have been secured in the boot bench they are automatically oriented correctly, and children can slip their feet into the boots without using their hands. Although the idea is simple, the measurements for the boot bench are critical. The angles shown in this drawing may not be exactly what your child needs. We suggest that you consult with your child's occupational or physical therapist so that the correct measurements and angles can be determined. For a better idea of how to make the boot bench, look at our drawing. Notice that the seat is deep enough so that the child sits on it sideways, and swivels to slip into the boots. It is important that no one step

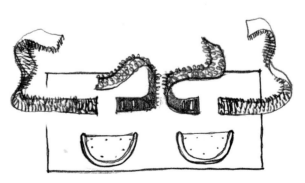

on the foot/boot support, since it is not designed to hold a child's weight.

Feeding and watering chickens

This chicken waterer with a built-up handle provides a good example of the usefulness of one of our favorite materials — pipe insulation. You can also use the same idea to design handles that will make other cumbersome items easier for your child to grasp. See "Measurements and Materials" for more information about pipe insulation.

Measure the circumference of the top and bottom of the waterer and add about four inches to each measurement. Using these measurements, cut two pieces of wire to size. We like to use inexpensive plastic-coated coat hangers. Wrap one of the pieces of wire tightly around the top of the chicken waterer and secure it in place by twisting the ends securely. Do the same with the other piece of wire, for the bottom of the waterer. Cut a piece of pipe insulation for the handle by measuring the distance from the twisted end of the bottom wire to the twisted end of the top wire, and adding two inches. Cut a piece of wire to match this measurement. Thread the wire through the pipe insulation and tightly twist the ends onto the top and bottom wire already in place on the

waterer. For safety, be sure the ends of the wire are not protruding. Wrap the handle with waterproof tape.

Feed Scoop

The scoop used by the child in our color illustration for carrying chicken feed is a plastic bleach bottle that has been thoroughly cleaned, and cut into the shape of a scoop. Scoops made of bleach or liquid detergent bottles are very handy for many types of animal feed, and are useful for many other things as well.

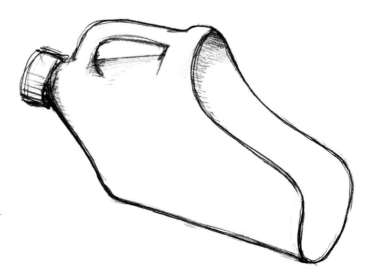

Easy-grip calf bottle

Another thing that can be difficult to hold on to is a calf bottle. Hungry calves butt and push enthusiastically. They are also likely to pull off the bottle's nipple in their eagerness to nurse, spilling the contents of the bottle all over themselves or your child. We've included a drawing of a homemade calf bottle holder that has been made of galvanized metal. Your child can use the bottle holder to grasp the bottle more easily with both hands. The holder has a hole for the nipple to pass through, so the nipple can't be pulled off. Tape can be placed on the calf bottle to indicate the right quantity of milk or milk replacer. A calf's grain can be carried in a lightweight plastic scoop like the one we talked about for chickens. Lightweight feed buckets can be used for the calf and can be hung with large, easy-to-grasp clips.

Caring for the family dog

Feeding and watering a dog can be a challenge for a child with limited mobility. Take a look at our color illustration. We've attached funnels to the doghouse at a height that a child can easily fill from a comfortable position. We used an oil change funnel (available at any automobile supply store) for water, and a plastic bleach bottle or liquid detergent bottle (thoroughly cleaned) for a funnel to feed the dog dry food. Be sure the mouth of the food funnel is large enough so that pieces of dry dog food don't get stuck in the opening.

Secure the food and water containers under the funnel. You can use wooden pegs to hold the dishes in place, fasten the containers to a board, or make a plywood stand with two recessed holes. An overhang on the doghouse protects the dog's food from rain. If your dog chews everything in sight, secure the funnels well, and protect them by wrapping them loosely with hardware cloth or odds and ends of metal screening.

Horseback riding

Horseback riding really deserves a chapter of its own! Riding a horse or pony is an exciting activity for any child, and riding programs for children with special needs have increased. Riding can provide children with a wonderful freedom of movement, and help with balance.

Custom-made riding aids

For a child who may have trouble grasping the reins, our drawing shows how to use a light-weight aluminum curb bit as a "rein handle." A more individualized solution for a child who cannot balance well is shown in our drawing. The rider in our color illustration is using a custom-made support that has been designed by Montana State University. Complete information about this support can be obtained from the Mechanical Engineering Department, Montana State University, Bozeman, Montana 59717. Attn: Dr. R. J. Conant. The child-support is attached to a plastic saddle pad.

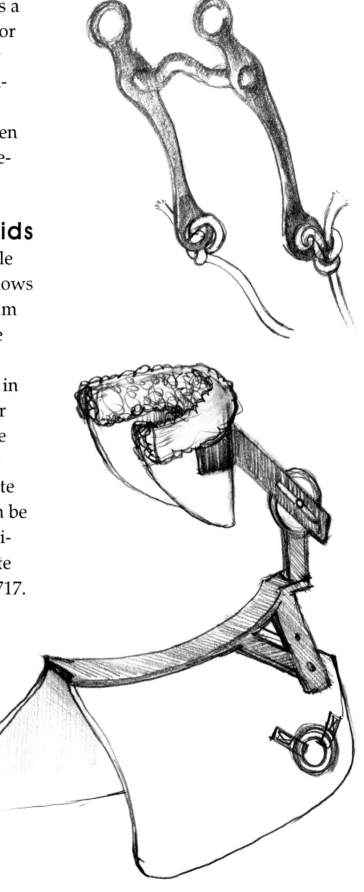

N.A.R.H.A.

There is a special (and very helpful) national association for horseback riders with disabilities. For complete information on safety features and equipment, we strongly encourage you to contact the North American Riding for the Handicapped Association (N.A.R.H.A.), P.O. Box 33150, Denver, Colorado 80233. Telephone (303) 452-1212.

Contact the NARHA for expert safety advice, and remember that certain things must be kept in mind to minimize risks while riding. Breakaway stirrups should be used so that a child's foot does not get trapped in case of an emergency. An approved riding helmet must be worn, and an experienced adult should supervise riding. Never tie, strap, belt, or in any way fasten a rider to the animal or equipment.

4-H involvement for your child

The mission of today's 4-H is to assist youth in acquiring knowledge, developing life skills, and forming attitudes that will enable them to become self-directing, productive and contributing members of society. 4-H programs are conducted throughout the United States. Urban as well as rural children are involved in 4-H projects ranging from aerospace to woodworking, animals to windowsill gardening. 4-H strives to find creative ways to integrate children with disabilities into traditional 4-H activities.

A recent publication by the Cooperative Extension Service of Purdue University can provide information about promoting integrated 4-H programs. Contact Breaking New Ground Resource Center, Purdue University, 1146 Agricultural Engineering Building, West Lafayette, Indiana 47907-1146. Ask them about "A Perfect Fit: 4-H Involvement for Youth with Disabilities."

There is a little girl named Jessica who has difficulty accomplishing many everyday tasks. Her parents and sisters have gotten so used to helping her do things that sometimes they don't think of teaching her how to do something by herself. Jessie lives on a farm. She loves to visit her pet goat in the barn, but she has to put on boots to be in the barn, and Jessie never could put her own boots on, so her sisters took turns putting them on for her.

One day, a friend of Jessie's mom was visiting the farm. She and Jessie's mom were sitting in the kitchen when they heard Jessie's sisters squabbling about who had to put Jessie's barn boots on for her. This friend was an occupational therapist and she started to think about ways that Jessie could learn to put her own boots on. Her thinking led to the "Boot Bench" that we've included in this book. By using the bench, Jessie learned to place a boot in the boot holder, and, without any difficulty, she could slide her foot right into her boot. Everybody was happy with Jessie's new skill, especially Jessie's sisters who no longer had to put Jessie's boots on for her.

A couple of months passed, and Jessie's mom's friend visited the farm again. She asked how Jessie was doing with her Boot Bench. "Oh, she never uses it." Jessie's mom reported. "Once Jessie learned that she could put her own boots on, she stopped using the Boot Bench. She still insists on doing it herself, but she has decided that the best place to put her own boots on is by sitting on the toilet seat!"

The point of this story is that assistive technology can be thought of as one stepping stone toward independence. Nobody says that a child has to use a piece of adaptive equipment forever. Our goal is to enhance a child's ability to perform a task. If, once the child gets the idea, she can move on and perform the task needing less support, that's fine too! The idea is — don't get stuck in a rut. Keep thinking of new ways to accomplish things, and encourage your child to think of new ways too. Experiment!

S. BLOOM '93

WHEELS

Wheels.... some children use chairs with wheels or walkers with wheels for mobility, some use riding toys with wheels for recreation; some children use wheels for both getting around and for playing. In any case, riding toys can provide hours of fun for any child. They provide youngsters with an opportunity to use large muscles and develop balance and coordination. When purchased through specialty catalogs, riding toys are often quite expensive. We would like to show you some examples of regular riding toys that have been adapted to meet the special needs of children, and some examples of homemade wheeled toys.

Tricycles

First let's talk about tricycles and bicycles. Sometimes a child's needs are best met by an adapted tricycle from one of the specialty catalogs, but sometimes homemade adaptations can be made that can modify a standard tricycle to your child's individual needs. Many parents have made their own modifications using their own ideas or "borrowing" ideas from catalogs, occupational and physical therapists, or specialized tricycles that their children use in school.

Vertical tricycle handlebar grips

Sometimes all a child needs are modifications for handlebars and

pedals such as the ones included in our color illustration. Vertical handlebar grips enable some children to steer more easily, and balance, on a tricycle. To change the handlebars to a vertical grasp, attach 4" pieces of 1" diameter dowel to the tricycle's standard handlebars using flat head screws and radiator clamps as shown in our drawing. Cover the dowel with pipe insulation or handlebar grips which can be bought in toy departments. Be sure to cover protruding sharp metal edges with waterproof tape.

Tricycle pedal foot-holders

To make a pair of tricycle pedal foot-holders, trace an outline of your child's shoe onto thin cardboard. Cut out the pattern about 1/2" outside the traced outline. Place this pattern on a tricycle pedal, and make a hole on either side of the central pedal rod. Cut two pieces of 1/2" plywood to match the pattern, and two rectangular plywood pieces the length of your child's foot pattern and 2" wide. Drill holes through both pieces to correspond to the holes in the pattern. Staple a curved piece of plastic for each foot-shaped piece as a heel support. We suggest using plastic from a liquid detergent jug because the plastic is easily workable, strong, and brightly colored. Cover the top side of the plywood with nonskid material such as a thin coating of silicone caulking.

Before bolting the top and bottom pieces of plywood together, securely staple a set of Velcro straps under the toe area, and another set across the ankle, positioned as shown in our drawing. Use carriage bolts to attach the top and bottom pieces of plywood to each pedal. We want to caution you that the pedal foot-holder prevents children from putting their feet down on the ground to stabilize themselves. When using escape-proof foot-holders of any type it's important not to let your child ride on uneven terrain. Also, your child should never ride unsupervised.

A child who is unable to use a modified foot-propelled tricycle may be able to use a hand-propelled tricycle which you may find in popular children's toy stores or catalogs.

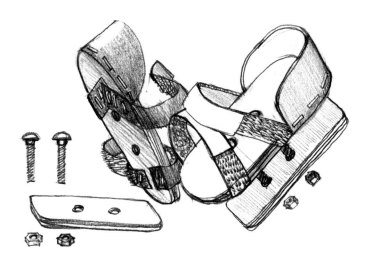

An electric tricycle

Engineering students at Tulane University have designed a creative tricycle solution. Plans for a motorized tricycle are available from Professor David A. Rice, Department of Biomedical Engineering, Tulane University, New Orleans, Louisiana, 70118. This vehicle, shown in our color illustration, is a regular tricycle with a child's bicycle passenger seat for support, and a small motor. The tricycle's front wheel is inserted into a slot in a board that resembles a skateboard.

There is a small electric motor and drive wheel on the board. Thus, the tricycle's front wheel is immobilized, and the power comes from the motor. Control is provided with a switch and a lever, both mounted on the handlebars.

Commercial electric cars

Another type of mechanized wheeled vehicle that can be adapted for individual children is the variety of electric cars sold in popular children's toy stores. Although we do not include these vehicles in this book, occupational and physical therapists, and engineers have thought of many simple control modifications that allow very young children the enjoyment of powered mobility. Talk to your child's occupational or physical therapist about adapting a commercially available electric car. If your child's control of such a vehicle is uncertain, you can wire in a power switch on a long cable, as shown in our drawing, so that you can cut the power off from outside the car if it should be necessary.

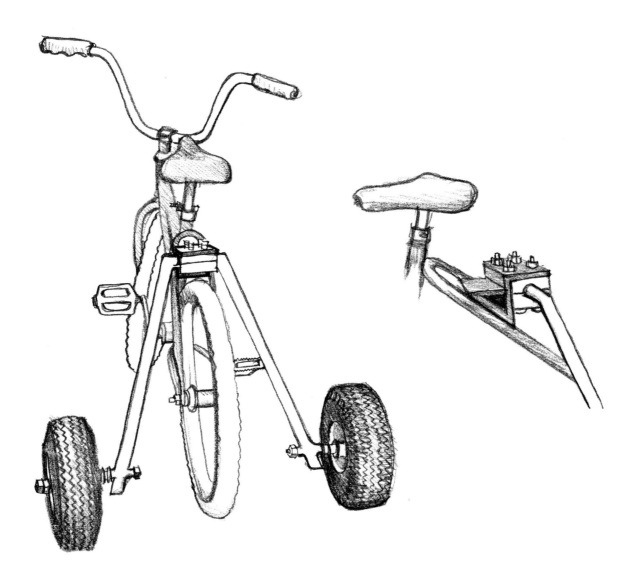

Permanent support wheels

A final comment about bicycles. To children, two-wheel bicycles are often a sign of growing up. However, to use a regular two-wheeler, a child must be able to balance well enough to use ordinary training wheels. If a child can handle the bicycle pedals and handlebars, but needs extra support to keep a bicycle upright, try making oversize, pneumatic-tired support wheels that can be permanently mounted on your child's regular bicycle and painted to match it. One example, designed by Cornell University engineering students, is illustrated here.

Walker/wagon

A homemade walker/wagon com-
bination might be just the right thing
for your child because it can be used
in a variety of ways. Children can use
the walker for assistance and at the
same time they can give their favorite
doll or stuffed animal a ride in the
"wagon." To make the walker/wagon,
cut down a used adult-sized walker,
or use a child's walker if you have
one. You can use old lawn mower
wheels or purchase new ones in your
local hardware store. (Tires and
wheels will be discussed later in this
chapter.) Attach two wheels to the
walker. Attach the other two wheels to
a small wooden box, or to a wood
base with a milk crate or laundry
basket mounted on it. Attach the
walker to the box with metal strapping, bolts, or U-bolts.

Scooter board

A homemade scooter board is a simple riding toy to make. The board, a piece of plywood covered with carpeting, provides a seat for the rider. The size of the board is determined by your child's size; a 16"x21" board works well for an average-sized eight-year-old. The scooter should be big enough for your child to balance on it easily. A child sits on the scooter, grasps the outer edges, and scoots! This is a sitting or "bellying" toy, not a standing one!

Making a scooter board is simple. Cover a piece of 3/4" plywood with carpeting and staple it to the underside of the board. Attach four swivel casters (2" diameter or larger — the larger the better!) about 2" in from the corners of the underside of the board. To prevent small fingers from getting hurt, don't mount the casters too close to the corners. If you want to be able to pull the scooter board, attach a screw-eye to the middle of the underside on one of the edges of the board, between the two front casters. A pulling rope can be attached to the screw-eye.

Wagon insert seat

Not all children can ride bicycles or tricycles, but every child wants to join in a "riding parade," and several other wheeled toys are shown in our color illustration. For example, wagons can enable children to participate in wheeled play. They are fun to pull and push, to load and unload. Express wagons with siderails can be purchased. Many have non-tip front steering. For children who need the support, an insert seat (described in the Garden chapter) can be bolted securely to the bottom of the wagon as shown in our drawing.

A word about wheels and tires

Now for a few final words on two important things that must be considered when you plan for rural children's wheeled toys — proper wheels and smooth, hard surfaces! In general, for rough terrain, pneumatic tires (tires filled with air) are better to use than hard rubber or plastic wheels; larger wheels are better than smaller ones, and "fatter" wheels are preferable to "skinny" wheels. Wheels can be purchased from your local hardware or farm supply store. If your hardware store doesn't stock the wheel you want, ask them to show you catalogs that you can order from. Of course, cost is a factor, and adequate wheels can often be taken from old, discarded lawn mowers, barbecues, baby carriages, etc. Very "bouncy" and "fat" balloon tires meant for uneven terrain have recently been advertised in magazines for families with children who have special needs.

Safety precautions

Wheeled toys do best on hard, smooth, surfaces. Unfortunately, the same hard surface that makes it easier to push, pull, or ride a wheeled toy, is also more likely to cause injury from a fall. So safety precautions are a must.

Notice that all of the riders in our color illustration are wearing bicycle helmets. Helmets are readily available at toy and bicycle shops. Please have your child wear one! Make sure that the helmet you buy is approved by ANSI (or Snell); the helmet will say if it's approved.

Ground surfaces

What outdoor surfaces are best for playing with wheeled toys? Usually, books about accessibility suggest "hard surfaces," as though we can all put black-top (asphalt) or concrete in our yards. Many of us can't, but grass, if it is carefully prepared and mown, can be very suitable for wheelchairs and wheeled toys. Historically, grass has been the smooth, hard surface of choice. Think of old-fashioned tennis courts, putting greens, and other playing greens that required smooth grass absolutely level, free from the slightest bumps, and covered with turf as smooth as velvet. You don't have to replace your entire lawn or backyard. If wheelchair accessibility is important, you can prepare specific areas or pathways of well-leveled, thickly seeded grass that you can keep mown short. A turfgrass area provides a firmer surface for walking and wheelchairs. It is less likely to erode, and in the long run will be easier to maintain. Talk to your landscaper, nursery, or

Cooperative Extension agent about the proper grass to plant for your climate and needs.

Gravel surfaces can also be useful to you for areas of wheelchair accessibility. However, if the stones are too large or too small it will be difficult to move the wheelchair. Sand and gravel dealers sell sifted bank-run gravel with only small stones and plenty of clay,

called "Item 4" which, if raked, packs down into a smooth, wheelchair-friendly surface. These dealers also sell "fine crusher run" — crushed stone and stone dust that packs down to a hard surface.

Finally, of course, there is blacktop or concrete, which are great for pathways, riding toys, driveways and wheelchairs.

Karen and her husband have a dairy farm, with lots of kids, dogs, kittens, and a lot of bustling activity on the summer day we visited with her. She had generously offered to take several hours (from her very busy schedule) to show us some of the homemade adaptive equipment she had made for her oldest daughter. So, we have recorded on film the charming accessible doll cradle that Santa made one year so that Sally in her wheelchair could play with her dolls. We have pictures of Sally in her homemade swing, and Sally hoeing her raised garden beds.

But the picture that is most memorable is a mental picture, a memory that Karen shared with us about Sally's first outdoor mobility device. Karen has always tried to provide Sally with many different outdoor experiences, so when Sally tried out her first outdoor wheelchair, Karen waited to see what she would do first. The memory that Karen has is that Sally went over to a tree to feel the bark. How can anyone have guessed that this little girl wanted to know what a tree felt like?

We can't guess everything that our children want to experience, and we know how hard it is to make backyards and rural settings accessible. Whether it's by letting your child crawl around in a strawberry patch, or using an insert seat in a wagon pulled by a friend, we hope our ideas in this book give you some ideas about how to enhance your child's outdoor play opportunities.

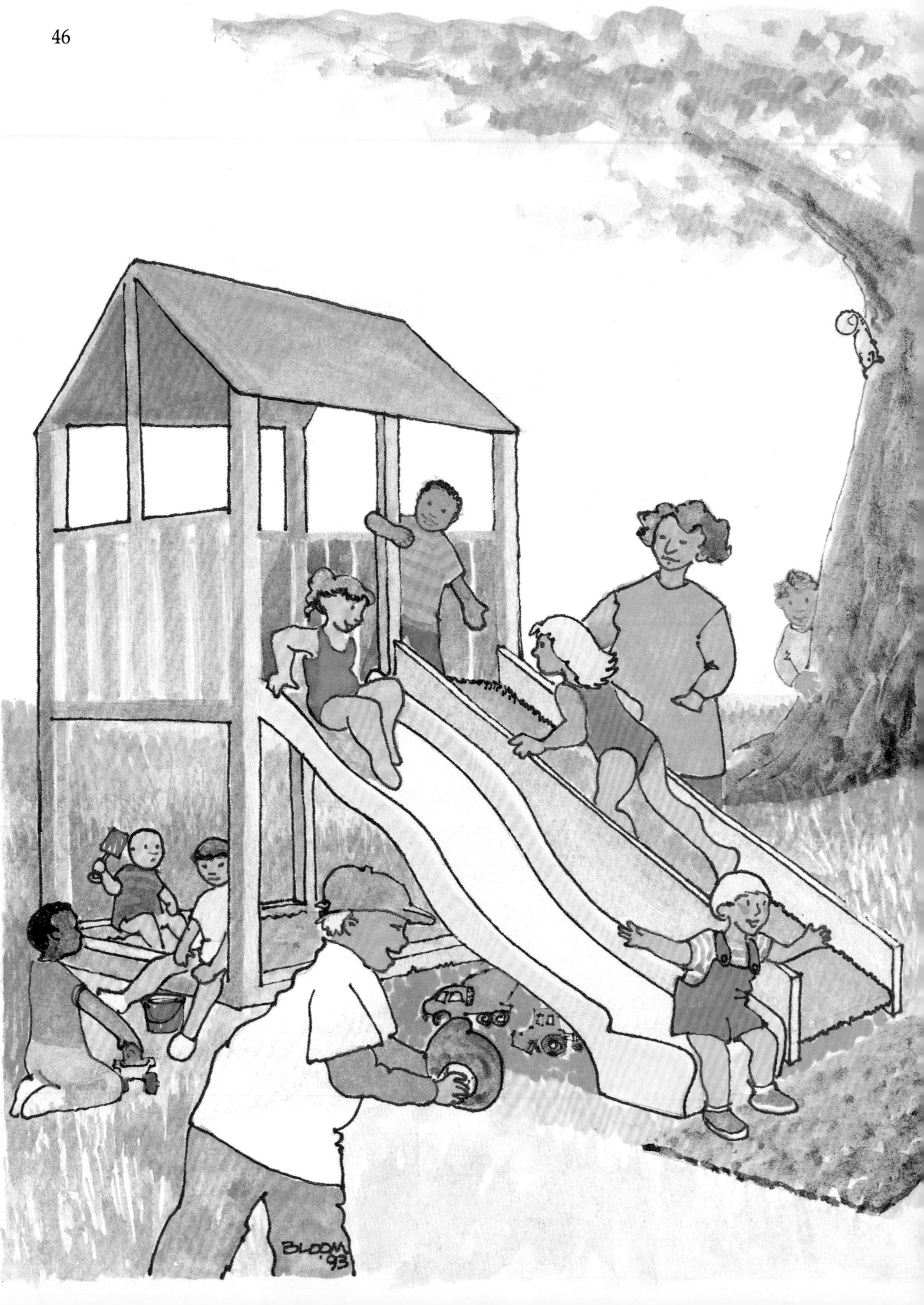
BLOOM '93

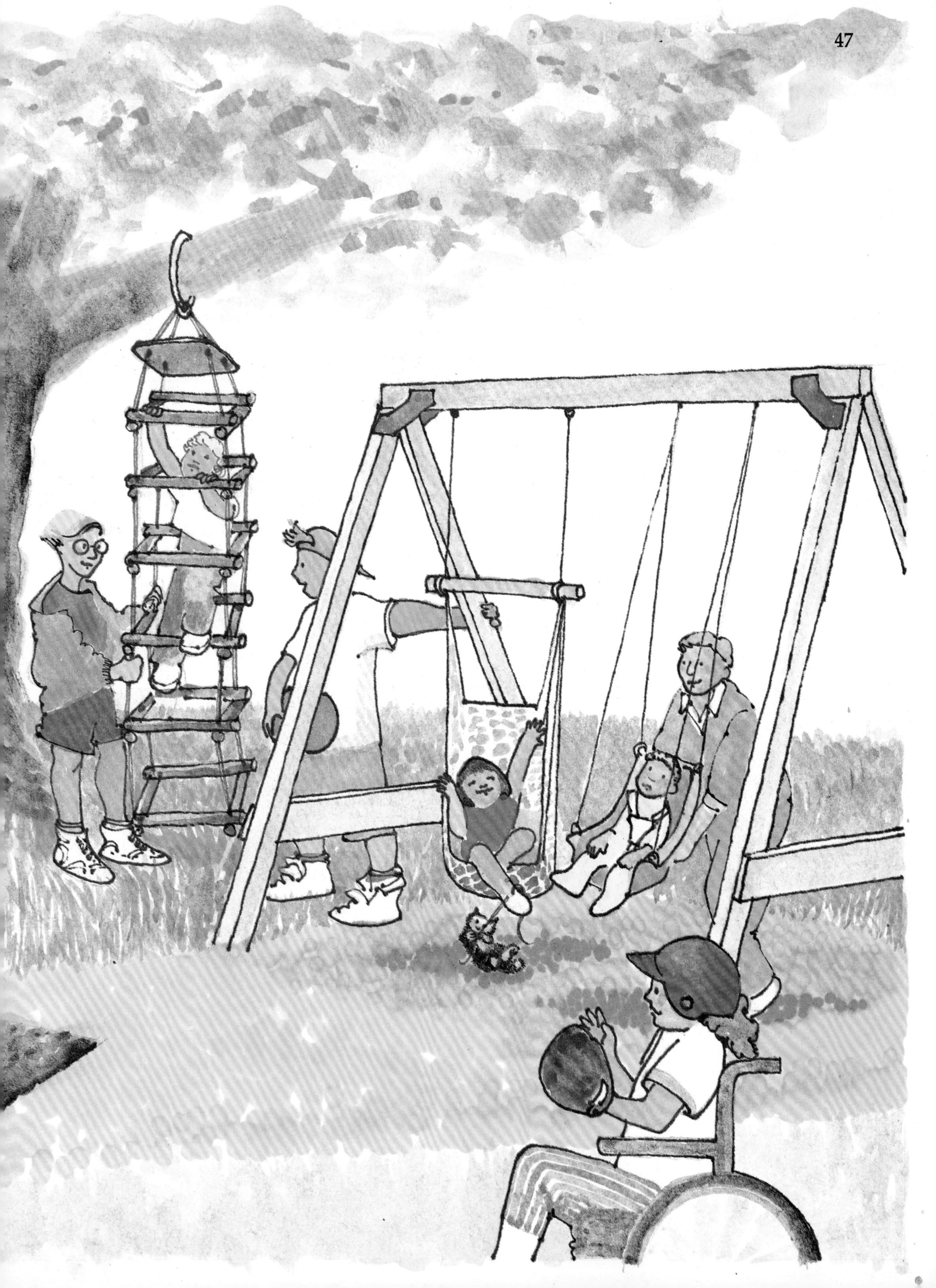

SWINGS & SLIDES

The child in all of us loves to play on a swing, take a quick ride down a slide, or dig in the sand. Outdoor play structures of one sort or another are found in almost every backyard, and in this chapter we will offer ideas about homemade equipment and accessibility that you can incorporate into your plans for your own backyard. Commercially available plans which include swings, slides, ladders, and sandboxes can also be adapted. Kits and plans are readily available through lumberyards and catalogs.

We are going to talk a lot about safety in this chapter because too many children get injured in playground mishaps that could have been avoided. Safety requirements do not eliminate flexibility, and we don't mean to discourage you. We just want to play safe!

Safety issues

Let's start with some of the "cautions and precautions." Choice of a location for outdoor play structures is critical. Choose a well-drained site, unless you enjoy mud and puddles. It should be close to the house so that it can be supervised, and away from vehicular traffic. You may want to fence in an area which would include outdoor play structures, riding toys, and a playhouse. See the "Backyard" chapter for fencing ideas.

There are some general guidelines that should be kept in mind when outdoor play structures are constructed. They must be durably built to withstand the weather. Solid foundations and anchoring are a must for these structures, and anchoring devices should be buried to prevent tripping. Platforms, balance beams, and suspension bridges should be placed close to the ground, to limit falling distance. Protruding bolts should be cut off flush with the nuts, smoothed, and covered with waterproof tape, rubber, or foam. Non-toxic treated lumber should be used, and splintery wood should be avoided. The equipment must be maintained in good condition.

A cushioned surface is a must for outdoor play structures. The soft surface should be wide enough to include falling distance. Sand, wood chips, or grass are good natural ground covers. Grass might be the best alternative for wheelchair access. Look at the "Wheels" chapter for information about planting grass for accessibility. While playing, children can also wear protective gear such as helmets, knee and elbow pads, long pants and long-sleeved shirts while playing.

Slide with ramp

Children are naturally attracted to slides, which are often the focal point of any play area. Because some children have difficulty climbing up ladders or stairs to reach the top of a slide, a ramp can be used, instead. In our color illustration, we included a ramp next to the slide so that children are able to get to the top without having to go all the way around to the back of the slide to climb up. The ramp's surface is covered with outdoor carpeting to prevent splinters and reduce slipping. Use treated boards instead of plywood to construct the surface of the ramp, so that moisture can drip through.

The flat platform at the top of the slide should be large enough so that a child can easily crawl from the ramp to slide. There should be railing all around the platform to prevent falls, especially since the platform will probably be used by children as a play area. The railing should be too high for children to sit on, and if wire fencing isn't used, the railing's vertical supports should be spaced so that children can't get their heads, arms, or legs caught.

The slide in our color illustration was purchased. There are no sharp edges because it is made of molded, hard plastic. The surface doesn't get too hot in the summer, and a lip at the end of the slide lessens the impact when a child comes off the slide. We placed rubber matting at the bottom of the slide to cushion the landing.

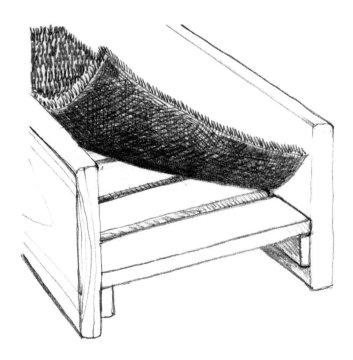

Hillside slide

As shown in our drawing, a slide can also be built into an embankment or hillside. This arrangement allows children to climb up the natural embankment to reach the top, and because the entire slide is close to the ground, there's less chance of injury.

Sandbox

A sandbox can be located under the ramp-and-slide platform. This location provides shade and protection from the weather. The sandbox in our color illustration is simply an anchored wooden frame filled with eight inches of playground sand. A sandbox can also be made from a plastic, child-sized swimming pool with drainage holes punched in the bottom. Remember to cover the sandbox when it's not in use. Otherwise, your cat or the neighbor's cat may think it's a great litter box!

Many sandbox toys can be adapted — for example, using Velcro (to help a child grasp a shovel) and pipe insulation (to make a built up handle for a small bucket). In fact, a sandbox itself can be adapted, using the plant table idea from our "Garden" chapter, for an accessible play area. Instead of sand, try using water, bird seed, or wood chips in the planting box containers.

Swings

Swings can be dangerous, yet they're often the first thing that children are attracted to in a play area. Swinging provides children with a wonderful sense of flying, and provides an opportunity for large muscle development. If your child has neurological involvement, be sure to check with your child's physician, or occupational or physical therapist to see if swinging, especially circular motion swinging, is an appropriate activity.

All swings require some type of permanent frame. You may have a large tree with a sturdy and healthy branch from which you can safely hang a swing. Or, you can build a permanent structure. Playing on a swing can be an indoor activity, as well. When inclement weather arrives a swing can be hung on a porch, or in the house. Whenever you hang a swing, allow enough space so that a moving swing can't hit other surfaces, or people.

Wooden-frame swingsets have become very popular, and many lumberyards and building-materials centers carry a full line of outdoor play structures and hardware. For safety, we suggest that you use commercially available hardware, following the manufacturers' recommendations.

Swing hardware

Materials used for attaching a swing to a support structure must be made of steel so they don't wear out too quickly or rust. All steel hardware should be galvanized. Closed swing hooks are better than open-ended ones, which can catch clothing or allow the swing to fall off. Closed swing hooks, already attached to a metal plate, are commercially available. If you do use an open-ended S-hook as part of your swing assembly, pinch the ends tightly with pliers after you attach the swing. Be sure to check hardware regularly. Chains are the sturdiest way to hang a swing; use chain that is at least 5/16". To prevent pinched fingers, cover the chain with pipe insulation or small-diameter garden hose. Plastic-covered swing chains are often included in purchased sets of swings.

Hammock swing

To make a hammock swing, purchase a hammock that doesn't have spreader bars. Get one with solid metal rings at each end. Tie knots at both ends of the hammock close to where the woven part attaches to the strings, taking care that the knot is on the woven part.

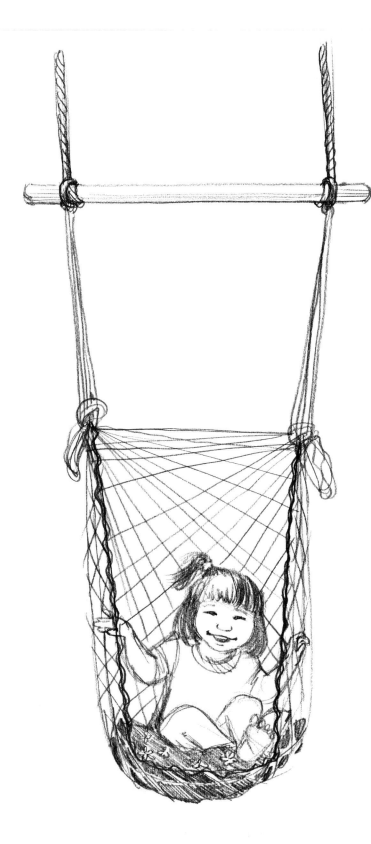

Cut a 3 foot long piece of dowel or broom handle with a diameter slightly smaller than the metal hammock rings. Screw an eye screw into the dowel about 6" from each end. This keeps the metal rings from sliding toward the middle. Secure the metal rings to the eye screws with tie-wraps.

Hang the swing, using the ropes that came attached to the hammock, with appropriate swing hardware. When the swing is hung, have an adult sit in it. Stand behind the swing and grasp the slack in the back edge with both hands. Bunch the excess hammock fabric as shown in our drawing. Tie the slack around the large knot you tied before at each end of the hammock. This will make a high back to the swing. We suggest that you weave a colored string through the front edge of the hammock swing so that you can find the edge more easily when the hammock swing in unoccupied. Cushions fit nicely in the hammock and help it keep its shape. Make sure to check the knots and hardware frequently.

Four-sided ladder swing

In our color illustration, we show a child climbing a homemade rope ladder made from plywood, lumber, and nylon rope. This four-sided ladder provides support and security so that a wide variety of children can have the chance to challenge their climbing prowess. Because the ladder has a single point of suspension, it can be hung from a tree as well as from a permanent play structure.

To make this ladder swing, measure the height that you want it to be and cut two lengths of 1/2" nylon rope about 3-1/2 times as long as the finished ladder's length. Thread the two ropes through a metal ring and knot them in the middle, so that you have four equal lengths to work with. Cut an 18" square piece of 1/2" outdoor plywood and drill 1/2" holes in all four corners for the rope to pass through. Cut 1" dowels or 1-1/4" closet rod into 18" lengths and drill 1/2" holes in each one 1-1/2" or 2" (on center) from each end.

In order to keep the knots and rungs level, you may want to suspend the swing and tie the knots as it hangs. The rungs are hung in "squares." Thread two parallel dowels, don't knot. Thread two more parallel dowels the opposite way. Tie an overhand knot in each of the four ropes under the dowels to make a square. Thread four more dowels in two parallel sets. Tie another four knots. On each rope, there should be twelve inches between the knots. Make sure you keep the rungs and knots even. When you are finished, the tails can either be cut off or kept on to anchor the swing to the ground.

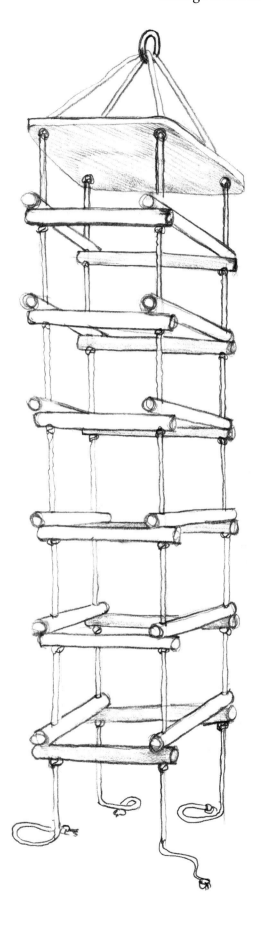

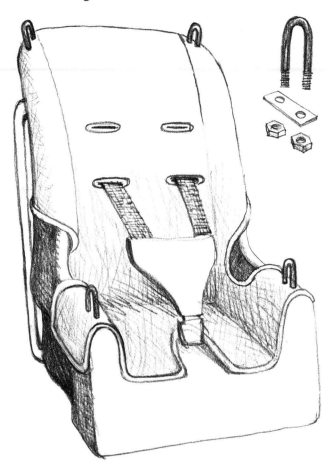

Car seat swing

Parents frequently ask us how to make a swing for small children who can't support themselves enough to use a regular toddler swing. Some parents have converted car seats into swings for their children. Car seats provide good support, they are equipped with safe harnesses, and can be very appropriate to use as swings for children who are small enough to fit comfortably.

However, we want to mention one caution about children, and one caution about equipment. Before you make a car seat swing, please talk with your child's occupational or physical therapist about whether swinging is an appropriate activity for your child and about the best hanging angle for the swing, because some children have developmental problems that make swinging inadvisable.

About the car seat itself — when we went shopping for used car seats to make prototypes, we found some car seats were so old that the plastic was brittle. Please make sure that the car seat you purchase to convert into a swing is in good condition before you invest your time and money.

To make this easy conversion, drill pairs of holes on both sides of the top and arms of the car seat. Insert U-bolts through each set of holes and secure them in place with locking washers and nuts on the underside of the car seat. Make sure you use U-bolts that are large enough to distribute the weight sufficiently. Before you swing your child in the swing, test it by using an object that is significantly heavier than your child.

Car seats come in a wide range of shapes, and some seats have narrow arms. Examine your individual car seat and determine the best way to drill and install eye bolts. You may need to adapt your method to your particular seat. Use appropriate swing hardware to suspend your car seat swing, and check all bolts and other hardware frequently.

A mother came to us with photographs of a swingset that she and her husband had built for their daughter. They had asked themselves how they could help their daughter enjoy a slide even though she couldn't walk around to a ladder or climb a ladder by herself. So they built a slide with a ramp next to it, covered the ramp with outdoor carpeting, and now their swingset is the "hit" of the neighborhood. It was a great idea, yet this woman's attitude was almost apologetic. She felt intimidated about sharing her ideas with us — after all we were the professionals, and she was only a parent.

If there's one thing we'd like to change for parents reading this book, it's the notion that only professionals can make decisions about assistive technology for children with special needs. Now, we're the first to suggest that parents and professionals collaborate to provide the best for each child, but we're also the first to suggest that parents have so much untapped creativity and know-how that they should "give themselves permission to be problem-solvers." Our suggestions to you parents are to:

- **Be creative** — Give yourself permission to try things. Look at catalogs and magazines for ideas (for example, there is a commercially available ramped slide/swingset that's been advertised in a well-known magazine). Use the C.A.S.E. strategy — Copy And Steal Everything. Keep a file of ideas for future use; exchange ideas with other parents.

- **Be safety-conscious** — Think of all the problems that <u>could</u> arise, and then think of creative ways to avoid those problems. Include railings to prevent falls, avoid spaces that can catch little arms and legs, eliminate sharp edges, use non-toxic materials, etc.

- **Be collaborative** — Use professionals' know-how, ask them questions, check your ideas with them for your child's specific needs. Talk to builders, tinkerers, engineers, as well as your child's occupational and physical therapists, and school staff.

S. BLOOM '93

OUR BACKYARD

Getting together for a picnic in the backyard — it seems particularly fitting, in our final color illustration, to show a family and friends preparing for a backyard celebration, a special time for the family to share a meal and enjoy each other's company. Here are some suggestions so that everybody can be included in the activities.

The back porch

Stairs are often a barrier for children and adults with limited mobility. You may have already constructed an accessible front entrance, but have you planned an accessible way to get to your backyard? It is also necessary for safety reasons to have a second accessible exit from a home in case of emergency. In our color illustration, we show a back door that opens to a multi-purpose porch. The back porch can be the area used for cleaning wheelchairs in inclement weather before bringing the wheelchair into the house. Installing an outside water faucet nearby can make this job a bit easier. Outdoor equipment and riding toys can also be stored on, or under, the porch.

Ramp specifications in rural settings

We'd like to talk specifically about ramps in rural settings. The 36" wide ramp in our color illustration has been built to match the uniform federal accessibility standards for adult-sized wheelchairs. Since the porch in our illustration serves as the wheelchair turning space, it has a clear space that is 60" in diameter. If our ramp were more than thirty feet long, we would have included a mid-ramp landing. Our ramp's slope has a rise of less than one foot over a distance of 12 feet. (One inch per foot.) This is the steepest slope that a ramp should have. An even more gradual rise of one foot over a distance of 20 feet may be more manageable for your child. Ramps and landings with drop-offs must have walls, railings or curbs (at least 2" high) to keep people from slipping or rolling off the edge of the ramp.

Remember that lighting is often poor in rural settings. Make sure that there is adequate outside lighting so that ramps and landings are well-lit.

Ramps in snowy and wet climates

Outdoor conditions in different climates require different ramp designs. All outdoor ramps should be designed so that water will not accumulate on the surface. All ramp surfaces should have non-slip surfaces. Porch/deck enamel is adequate if you liberally sprinkle playground sand on it when it's freshly painted. In snowy climates expanded metal grating works well as a ramp surface because there is no snow build-up on the ramp itself. Plastic storm-window material can also be stapled along the handrail on the ramp's outer edge to keep blowing snow off the ramp. Make sure the ramp is not under your roof's overhang so that rain and melting snow will not pour down on it. Either build the ramp out from the house a bit or build a roof over the ramp.

Handrails on ramps

Handrails, running continuously along both sides of the ramp, should extend a foot beyond its top and bottom. To make the handrails easy to grip, there's a 1-1/2" space between the handrails and the wall. The handrails do not rotate within their fittings. Handrails should be installed at an appropriate height for your child. We suggest two sets of handrails — one for your child and the other set at 34"

above the ramp surface, for adults. Our ramp also has a flat, concrete pad at the base of the ramp and a smooth-surfaced, firm pathway that leads away from the ramp.

Fences: types and uses

In our color illustration of the family's backyard, you'll notice a variety of fences. Fences can be used to define an area for a backyard activity, but they should not be counted on to be the sole protection for children who need adult supervision. A fence may delay a child's escape, but can't be relied on to prevent it! Children can be surprisingly clever in learning to climb fences and unlatch locked gates. A child can easily wander through a gate that hasn't been tightly secured. Likewise, a fence can't always keep dangers out!

Given these realities, we're including information on fences and gates because they can be helpful in some situations. If you're spending time in an area with your child, a fence can serve as added protection. For children who run exuberantly, a fence can be the barrier that prevents a tragedy. Fences can also help visually impaired children to orient themselves.

Before enclosing an area, be sure that the area is large enough to be stimulating for your child. Provide enough activities in the area so that your child will want to play there. If you're trying to fence off a potentially dangerous area, such as a ravine or driveway, explain to your child why the fence is being built. There are many commercially available fences; you'll have to decide which is best for your child. There are advantages and disadvantages to each. One of the most durable is a chain-link fence. Vinyl-covered chain-link is rust-proof. The posts for a chain-link fence are expensive and must be set in concrete. And, a note of caution: this type of fence does provide easy toe grips for a child who's an agile climber.

You can build your own fence from woven vinyl-covered wire and fence posts. This type of fence is not as attractive or as permanent as some others, but it's less expensive. Another relatively inexpensive option is a snow fence. The newer plastic fencing is better than the older wooden variety. Space the fence posts closely, to ensure rigidity, and use tie wraps to fasten the fencing to the posts.

Wooden fences are usually bought in sections. Be careful to select a fence with narrow openings between the slats to prevent young feet and hands

from getting caught. Splinters can also be a problem. However, remember that for safety reasons, any enclosed area, whatever it's fenced in with, should have an exit. This will require you to construct a gate and choose a latching device. There are many commercially available latches. Consult your lumber yard or hardware store. As we pointed out, children can be very adept at opening latches, and parents sometimes forget to close gates securely. A possible solution is to install an electronic signal device that will tell you if a gate has been opened. These devices are relatively inexpensive to purchase and install. Not all fences are built, some are grown. Depending on the purpose of your fence, a natural barrier can serve as a boundary. A close planting of small shrubs can be aesthetically pleasing and also serve to enclose an area.

Accessible picnic table

A backyard barbecue should be an inclusive occasion with everyone in the group able to sit at the picnic table together. Our color illustration shows a few ways in which picnic tables can be accommodated to individual's seating needs. One way to make sure that a person using a wheelchair can sit at the picnic table is to build an accessible table. A simple picnic table can be built with an extra overhang at one end so that a wheelchair can comfortably fit underneath. The same guidelines that you would use in making your kitchen table accessible, like clearance space underneath the table, can be used to determine the height of your homemade picnic table. Make sure there are no rough surfaces, and no bolts sticking out to avoid injuries.

Picnic table extension

An easy way to make a commercially purchased picnic table accessible is to attach a simple plywood extension to the table. Cut a 24 inch piece of 3/4" plywood the same width as your table. Fasten the plywood to the top or bottom surface of your picnic table with carriage bolts. There should be ample clearance for your child's wheelchair to roll easily under the extension. It is easy to make the extension the right height for your family member by inserting spacing boards between the table and the plywood. Use outdoor quality plywood and paint it or seal it for durability.

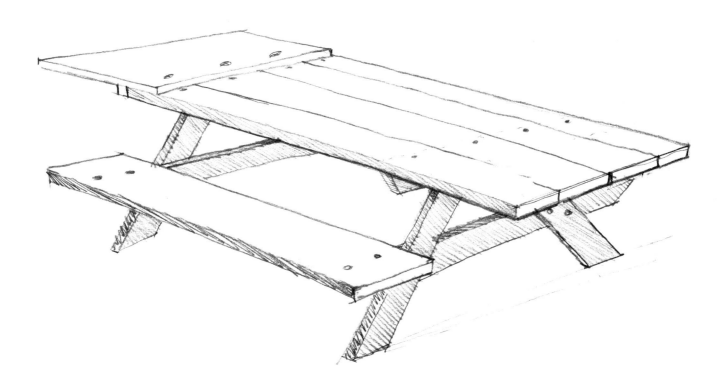

Swivel seat for picnic table

If your picnic table and bench are attached to each other, and the bench is the right height and distance from the table top for your child, you can attach a swivel seat to the picnic bench. Make a simple swivel seat by taking two squares of plywood as shown in our drawing and securing them through the picnic table bench with a carriage bolt, washers, wing-nut and locking nut. Securely fasten an insert seat to the top plywood. Situate the swivel base near the middle of the bench for stability. You can place your child in the seat, fasten whatever support straps are necessary, and then swivel the child around to face the picnic table. For safety, only do this with a picnic table that has the benches connected to it.

There are also commercially available swivel bases that people use when they make bar-stools. The swivel bases can be found in home carpentry catalogs.

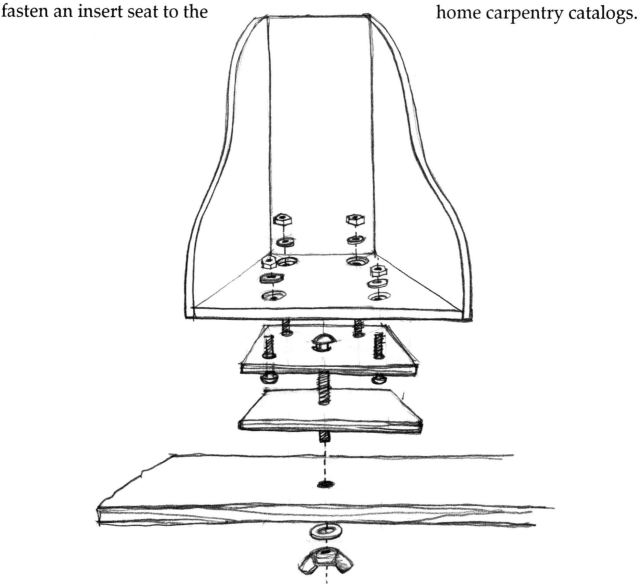

Adirondack chair

An Adirondack chair is a comfortable and enjoyable seat for children. It is very stable and well-balanced, and it fits in well with other backyard furniture. Because of the chair's sloped back and seat, a child who has little trunk control can often sit independently without support. Detailed plans for building Adirondack chairs are widely available. The chair back should be high enough to support your child's head, and your child's feet should reach the ground. It is important for your child to be well fitted to the seat. You can modify the plans by changing the angle between the seat and the back if you need to adjust the positioning for your child, but consult your occupational or physical therapist before you make design changes. If the Adirondack chair is more than a few inches wider than your child, use lateral pillows for support.

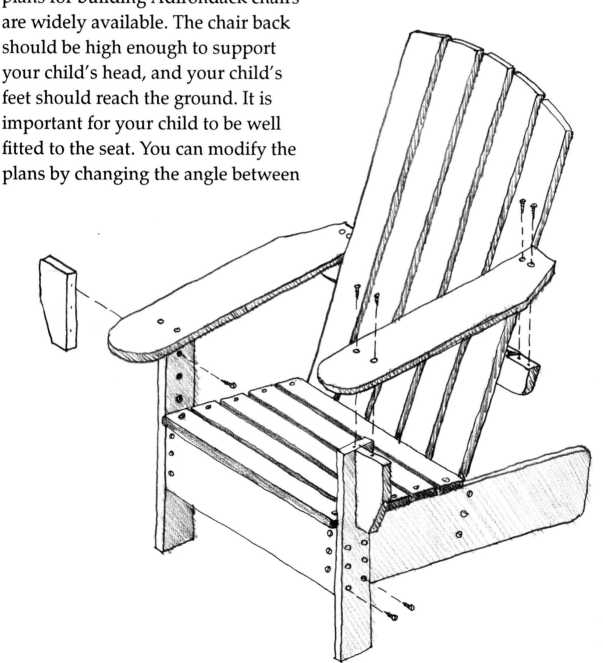

Inclusion/Conclusion

After reading the chapters in this book, it should come as no surprise that we believe fervently that children should be involved in their families' activities. At the same time, we definitely do not mean to communicate the message that you are not doing enough with/for your children, or that it is somehow your responsibility to do "more" with your children.

All too frequently each of the professionals working with an individual child says to a parent, "You should spend a half hour every day doing such-and-such." ....each child's speech therapist, and occupational therapist, and physical therapist, and teacher, each prescribing an additional half hour of responsibility to already overburdened parents. That just leads to guilt.

Our message is that sometimes it's the environment that creates barriers, not children's functional limitations. And sometimes it's possible, with a little bit of imagination, and a little help from a friend (your neighbor with a woodworking shop, your relative who is an avid gardener, your dad who just retired, the neighborhood Mr. Fix-it) to "fix-up" the environment a little bit, to help you make it a little bit more accessible to your child's special needs.

We have tried to share our enthusiasm for a "do it yourself" approach to assistive technology problem-solving. We've told you about some of our favorite, ordinary materials that can be used to make things for individual children. We've been positive and practical. We hope that we've made this book fun to use as a resource. Many of the ideas in this book originated with parents we've worked with. We would very much appreciate hearing from you and any ideas that you've had.... maybe something you've made, or something you've thought of, but haven't made. Please tell us, and we will share the information with other parents. We can be reached at:

New York State Rural Health and Safety Council
324 Riley-Robb Hall
Cornell University
Ithaca, NY 14853-5701
Voice (607) 255-0150; **TTY** (607) 255-1143
FAX (607) 255-4080

MEASUREMENTS

On this page, we show how to measure your child. These drawn directions are deliberately simple. If your child requires individual positioning, please consult with your child's occupational or physical therapist. Our directions are meant to assist you in making furniture height accessible for your child, and in making things wide enough for comfort. We do not want to suggest that your measurements can replace a professional's skilled seating and positioning information.

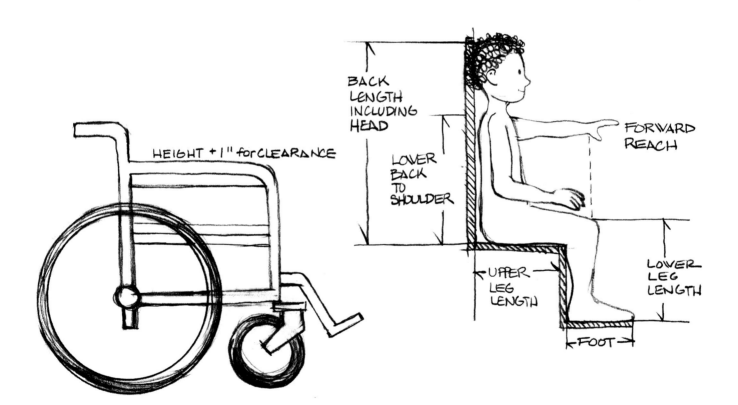

MATERIALS

We've been vague about materials because we want you to use whatever you have around. These projects are things for you to make at home. We're not suggesting the use of plastic detergent jugs in schools or public playgrounds! Our list of materials includes some of our favorites. Add your own, substitute materials you have around. Please remember: Safety is the first consideration!

On the following pages we will describe some of our favorite construction materials. The experts to consult about everyday materials are your lumberyard staff, the people who work at your local hardware store, and, if you're lucky enough to have one, your neighborhood "Fix-it" person.

Balls

Tennis balls, racquetball balls, and hollow plastic golf balls are our favorites, because they can be slit or cut to make built-up knobs and grips, and can be glued in place if necessary. Tennis balls also make good coverings for sharp nails (hanging buckets in garden). They will stand up well to the weather. We don't suggest using "nerf" or foam balls because they can be chewed or picked apart. As a safety precaution, make sure the ball you use is larger than will fit in your child's mouth.

Bolts/screws/nuts/washers

Talk to your local hardware store or lumberyard if you have questions about what bolts and screws are appropriate for a project. Remember that some bolts have flat heads, others have round heads, and each has its own use. A sharp bolt or screw head or end can easily scratch your child, so if there are exposed bolt heads or ends, cover with tape or pieces of pipe insulation for protection. Make sure that you are using the appropriate nuts and washers. If you don't have much experience with making homemade projects, talk to someone in your community who can help. This drawing of different bolts and screws may help you get started.

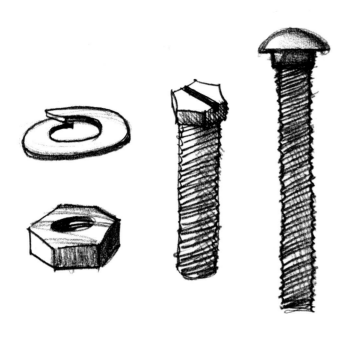

Buckets/containers/ scoops

Heavy plastic buckets are sometimes available very inexpensively, or free, at restaurants, bakeries, or supermarkets. Make sure the bucket is thoroughly clean and do not use a bucket that once held non-food, or possibly toxic materials. Holes can be drilled in buckets, and they can be cut with a coping or hacksaw. Plastic buckets make good planters, but there are many other uses as well.

Smaller plastic containers are also useful. Avoid using very flimsy or non-food containers. Small plastic containers can have handles attached to make small buckets. They can be used for berry buckets and for heel supports on the boot bench. Containers can be cut with a coping saw or heavy duty shears. Sharp edges should be smoothed with sandpaper or an emery board.

Plastic bleach and detergent bottles can be converted into scoops. Cutting is easily done with shears. Make sure that the bottles have been thoroughly cleaned before using.

Dowels

Dowels can be found at lumberyards, hardware stores, or craft stores. They come in a wide variety of diameters and can be expensive. Commercial dowels are usually made out of hardwood and can be difficult to drill or cut. That's why when we say "dowel," we really mean round long rods or sticks, because sometimes it is possible to use a straight tree branch or a discarded broomstick instead of a commercially purchased wooden dowel. Remember when choosing your dowel to take into consideration the strength needed and the weight that the dowel will add to the object. Sometimes it's better to use a smaller diameter dowel and build up the handle at the end using lightweight foam instead of using a heavier dowel for the whole length.

Glues

Selecting the right glue is important because it can be very frustrating if your project falls apart. Local hardware stores are often a good source of information about what specific glue to use. In general, epoxies, where you mix two separate ingredients, work best. We've found that some plastics are difficult to glue, so always test a sample before committing yourself to the final project. Don't forget there are specialty wood glues. Remember, as a safety measure, to periodically check glued surfaces for security.

Handles/knobs

Look around, and use your imagination. You can make handles out of empty thread spools, blocks of wood, wire covered with tape and/or pipe insulation — almost anything that your child can grasp easily. Remember, metal handles can be cold to handle in the winter. The size and shape of a handle will depend on your child's size, grasp, and strength. Consult with your child's occupational or physical therapist if you are uncertain about what handle would be best in a given situation.

Lumber/plywood

Check your local lumberyard for specifics if you don't know what type of plywood or lumber you need for a project. Plywood comes in a variety of thicknesses and quality and can be expensive to purchase. Sometimes lumberyards have inexpensive plywood scraps. If you need a small piece of plywood for a project, check with a hardware store or lumberyard before you buy a 4'x8' sheet of plywood. A local building contractor can sometimes be a good source of scrap lumber, and can also provide technical advice. Remember to use exterior grade plywood so that you can be sure that it will stand up to the elements. Make sure your treated lumber and plywood is non-toxic. Sand all rough edges and cover with nontoxic paint or sealer.

Pipe insulation

Hot water pipe insulation is available in two diameters at your local plumbing or hardware stores. It is a very inexpensive alternative to specialty foam tubing. Generally black or gray, pipe insulation looks better if you cover it with colorful waterproof tape. In previous chapters, we frequently suggested using pipe insulation as a way to make or build up

handles (chicken waterer). Make sure you don't use it with children who will chew on it. Pipe insulation is slit along its length. Pipe insulation can also be used to pad sharp corners. If the diameter is too large for your purpose, you can cut it down to size and wrap it securely with waterproof tape.

Plastic

Occupational and physical therapists use sophisticated plastics that soften in hot water and can be molded to fit a child's individual need. We haven't discussed thermal plastic in this book. Instead, we described ways to use plastic that was available from discarded and recycled jugs, buckets, lids, and whatever else we could find that met our needs. Our favorite source is the plastic from large liquid laundry detergent jugs because it is very easy to work with. You can cut it

with scissors, but it has enough strength to be useful in a variety of ways. You can staple through it. And it comes in such a nice variety of pretty colors!

Radiator hose clamps

Radiator hose clamps can be used to hold a variety of things together. Available at automobile and hardware stores, they come in many sizes. If you are purchasing a radiator hose clamp, get one that isn't too long for the project. As you make things, you will discover how handy these clamps can be. Make sure you wrap the clamp completely with tape because its edges are sharp.

Silicone caulking, and nonslip surfaces

You can get silicone caulking in your local hardware store, lumberyard, or plumbing store. It comes in a tube, and is generally either white or clear — or blue if you buy it as RTV gasket compound in an automobile supply store, which is the cheapest form we've found. Silicone caulking is one of the most versatile nonskid materials because you can apply it in lines or dabs, or spread thin coatings to provide a nonskid surface. It will adhere to most surfaces. Use a few dabs on the bottom of plates or cups to keep them from sliding on the table. We have mentioned its possible uses only a few times, but you will find it has many applications, and we encourage you to be creative.

Another non-skid material is carpet backing which can be bought in rolls at any carpet or department store. It is a very flexible open-weave netting with plastic coating, and can be glued to surfaces for permanent application.

Tie wraps

Tie wraps are readily available in hardware stores. Tie wraps are plastic strips with a one-way locking mechanism. They come in various lengths, widths, and colors. We've indicated their use to secure things together, such as dowels to handles. Remember, once the tie-wrap is pulled tight, it cannot be released without cutting it off. Please make sure that you trim the excess length of plastic strip once the tie wrap is in place, and that you round the cut end or cover the end with tape to make it smooth.

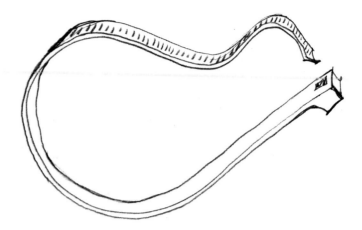

Velcro

Velcro can be bought in fabric stores, department stores, hardware stores, and even in large supermarkets. Velcro is a fastening material made up of two types of surfaces: a hook side and a loop side. It's an alternative to buttons, snaps or zippers. Velcro comes in many widths, colors, and shapes, with adhesive or nonadhesive backing. We've found that the adhesive doesn't hold very well. Velcro can be sewn or glued on. The hook side of Velcro collects lint and needs to be occasionally defuzzed.

In previous chapters, we've mentioned ways to use Velcro for securing straps and for adjustable handles, but it can also be used to replace buttons or snaps on clothing. Please be careful when using Velcro on seating straps; it makes a quick release strap but may not hold securely enough. Talk to your occupational or physical therapist if you are planning to use Velcro for seating modifications.

Waterproof tape

Plastic waterproof tape comes in many colors and widths, and can be purchased at supermarkets, department stores, and hardware stores. Please don't use it with children who chew on inedible things. We've noted its use when wrapping pipe insulation to make handles. It can also be used to join things together, and for decoration. It can be used to cover sharp edges, or wire, but please be sure that you have wrapped it around enough times to adequately pad the sharp edge.

Webbing

Be selective in the webbing widths that you use. Velcro can easily be sewn to webbing to make quick-release straps, which are useful in case of emergency. Make sure that the strap is appropriate for the job and that it will hold. Consult with your child's occupational or physical therapist about harness design and dimensions. Remember that improper straps can be hazardous.

Wire

Wire can be bought in a variety of local stores in a wide array of diameters and flexibility. We often use coat hanger wire to make handles. Coat hangers come in a range of stiffness; some projects require stiffer wire. Pliers are often helpful in bending stiff wire. Cutting wire always leaves a sharp end, so make sure it gets filed and well-covered with tape or padding, a small piece of pipe insulation works well, too.

To order this book, or for information on our other publications relating to children with disabilities, please call or write:

Brookline Books
P.O. Box 1047
Cambridge, MA 02238-1047

(617) 868-0360
Fax: (617) 868-1772
Within the U.S.: 1-800-666-BOOK
E-mail: brooklinebks@delphi.com